GW00359669

THE ENVIRONMENTALLY
FRIENDLY GARDEN

GARDEN MATTERS
THE ENVIRONMENTALLY FRIENDLY GARDEN

ALAN TOOGOOD

WARD LOCK

First published in Great Britain in 1991
by Ward Lock Limited, Villiers House,
41/47 Strand, London WC2N 5JE, England

A Cassell Imprint

© Ward Lock

Line drawings by Mike Shoebridge

Text filmset in ITC Garamond
by Columns Design and Production Services Ltd., Reading
Printed and bound in Glasgow
by Collins

British Library Cataloguing in Publication Data
Toogood, Alan R. *1941–*
The environmentally friendly garden.
1. Gardening
I. Title II. Series
635.0484
ISBN 0–7063–7027–9

CONTENTS

Preface   6

PART 1: GROWING CONDITIONS FOR PLANTS
1 Soil improvement   9
2 In the greenhouse   21

PART 2: PLANT CARE
3 Mulching   29
4 Feeding plants   34
5 Watering plants   40
6 Pest and disease control   46
7 Weed control   55

PART 3: GARDEN FEATURES AND PLANTS
8 Miscellaneous features   61
9 Plants and their conservation   67

**PART 4: SAFETY AND COMFORT IN THE
   GARDEN**
10 Smoke and noise   72
11 Machinery and equipment   78
12 Problem plants   84

PART 5: WILDLIFE
13 Attracting wildlife   87

Index   94

PREFACE

Protecting the environment is uppermost in many people's minds today. We are shocked when we learn from television and radio news bulletins, and from newspapers and magazines, the extent to which our modern way of life is damaging the environment, wildlife and even people. So we are being urged to think and act 'green' by various organizations and institutions, including the Government and even by a member of the royal family.

One would think that gardening is completely in harmony with the environment, a harmless pastime causing no problems to anyone or anything, but unfortunately this is not so.

Gardeners are among the main users of a non-renewable resource, peat – so much so that there is growing concern for the future of peat bogs (unique wildlife habitats) in Britain, even though peat producers are setting aside conservation areas. Some people and organizations are now starting to feel that it is morally wrong to extract peat, and there are numerous alternatives to peat for soil improvement, potting composts, etc, explored in this book. Some are already well known, but others are very new.

Caring for plants can make heavy demands on natural resources, including water. Garden watering undoubtedly contributes to the water shortages which seem all too common now in some parts of Britain, where spring and summer bans on garden watering are the norm. This, coupled with the fact that water is becoming ever more expensive, and with metering on the cards, it is more important than ever today to conserve water. Ways of achieving this in the garden are therefore explored.

Today, many people do not like using chemicals for

feeding plants nor for pest, disease and weed control, for fear of polluting the soil and harming wildlife. Alternative controls are considered in this book. We also use numerous non-renewable materials for constructing our gardens, but there are alternative, readily available renewable materials that one could consider.

Safety and comfort in the garden must be considered by all of us: how many of us detest smoky bonfires and excessive noise from neighbours, especially on a pleasant summer's afternoon when we want to relax in the garden? Yet both are completely unnecessary.

Plants can damage our health – especially those which are poisonous (a real problem with small children in the family) or those which cause allergies. Learn here about those to avoid. While on the subject of plants to avoid, do consider the guidelines on avoiding buying plants which have been collected from the wild, as uninhibited collection has resulted in many plants being on the verge of extinction in their native habitats.

The environmentally friendly garden will actively encourage wildlife, such as butterflies, bees, frogs, and small mammals. You will find in these pages how to create the right conditions for these animals and which plants to grow.

For many readers all of this may amount to new ways of gardening, but you will find your gardening just as enjoyable as it has always been – perhaps even more so in the knowledge that your plot of land is in harmony with the environment.

A.T.

PART 1

GROWING CONDITIONS FOR PLANTS

CHAPTER 1

SOIL IMPROVEMENT

Soil improvement requires the incorporation of bulky organic matter, but if a renewable form is used then the heavy demands need not create an environmental problem. Peat is often recommended for soil improvement but is non-renewable (consisting of decomposed sphagnum moss or sedges extracted from bogs), so you may wish to consider alternatives.

BULKY ORGANIC MATTER

Bulky organic matter, incorporated into the soil during digging, improves the texture and fertility of the soil, and eventually decomposes into beneficial humus (completely decayed organic matter). The addition of such organic matter is recommended for many soil types, including clay, where it helps to open up this sticky soil, so improving drainage of rainwater. Conversely, organic matter helps free-draining soils like sands, gravels and chalk to hold on to moisture and plant foods, since it acts like a sponge.

HOW TO USE

The organic matter is added to the trenches while digging, at a rate of at least one level barrowload per

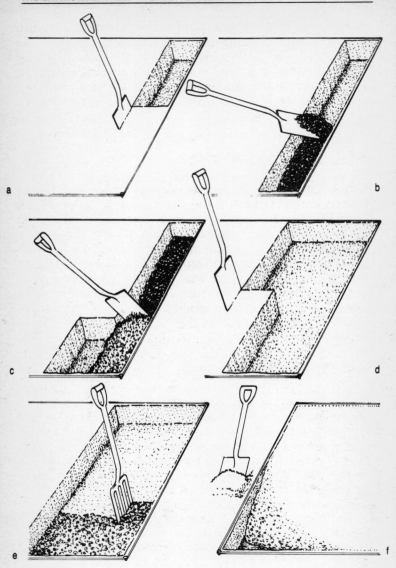

a

b

c

d

e

f

4 sq m (4 sq yd), or one bucketful per square metre (square yard). Digging is carried out regularly on the vegetable plot and beds used for bedding plants, generally in autumn, and it should always be carried out prior to planting permanent plants, as when preparing a mixed border, or when preparing a site for a new lawn (Fig. 1).

MODERN ALTERNATIVES

A new alternative to peat is coconut fibre (coir fibre) from coconut husks. It is the short waste fibres and husk particles that are used as a peat alternative (the long ones being used for coconut matting, rope making, etc.). It is very similar in texture and appearance to sphagnum moss peat and retains moisture well. It is interesting to note that coconut fibre was used in gardening to a limited extent in the nineteenth century but for some reason it never became popular, presumably because peat was later accepted as the ideal soil improver.

Pulverized or shredded bark is a relatively new material. For adding to the soil during digging partially composted (or decomposed) bark is better than 'raw'

Fig. 1 *Bulky organic matter is added to the trenches while digging. With 'normal' or single digging (a and b) each trench is 45 cm (18 in) wide and 30 cm (12 in) deep. Soil from the next trench is thrown forwards into the preceding one (c). Deep or double digging (d) is recommended for previously undug ground and when preparing ground for permanent planting. The trench is 60 cm (2 ft) wide and 30 cm (12 in) deep and the organic matter is incorporated while digging the bottom of the trench to the depth of a fork (e). Soil from the next trench is again thrown forwards into the preceding one and the last trench is filled with soil removed from the first (f).*

bark. This is readily available as a proprietary product from garden centres. Bark is especially good at opening up heavy clay soils to improve their drainage.

TRADITIONAL BULKY MATERIALS

Garden compost is highly recommended as it costs virtually nothing to make and contains plant foods. How to make it is described below. Home-made leafmould is also a good source of bulky organic matter but low in plant foods. It is easy to make at home.

Just as good, or even better than garden compost, are farmyard manure and stable manure, which may be difficult to obtain in some areas. They are not expensive and contain plant foods, but these manures must be rotted down before digging them in as fresh manure can cause damage to plants. Make a heap in a covered area (or cover the heap with a polythene sheet) for several months until it is partially decomposed. These manures may contain wood shavings – another reason why they must be composted before use, as raw shavings can deplete the soil of nitrogen, a major plant food, in the course of decomposing.

Used mushroom compost (obtainable from mushroom growers) is decomposed horse manure and contains chalk, so it is not recommended if you do not want to increase the chalk content of your soil. This material is comparatively cheap and contains some plant foods.

Spent hops are a by-product of breweries and are quite cheap to buy, provided you live near a brewery. Hops should be stacked and allowed to rot down before use, as for farmyard or stable manure.

MAKING GARDEN COMPOST

This is not only a good way of getting rid of garden rubbish but also provides one of the best forms of bulky organic matter. Once rotted down, suitable garden rubbish assumes a brown crumbly texture, which can take from three to eight months, depending on temperatures and materials used.

CONSTRUCTING A CONTAINER

The heap is best made in a shady, warm, sheltered part of the garden – but out of sight! Make a bin of some kind to contain the materials. It should be as large as possible, at least 1 m (3 ft) in each direction, but not more than 1.2 m (4 ft) high, as the bigger the heap the quicker the composting process.

A simple container could be a square or rectangular wire-netting enclosure, the netting supported with stout timber corner posts. Cover with a sheet of black polythene to keep off the rain (otherwise you will end up with a soggy slimy mess). Wire netting allows good air circulation through the heap, which aids decomposition. One side or end of the enclosure should be removable to allow you to remove the compost easily.

A more sophisticated compost bin can be constructed of slatted timbers and fitted with a sloping lid on the top. Removable slats in front will allow you to dig out the compost (Fig. 2).

There are also various proprietary compost bins on the market if you prefer, many being ideally suited to small gardens (Fig. 3).

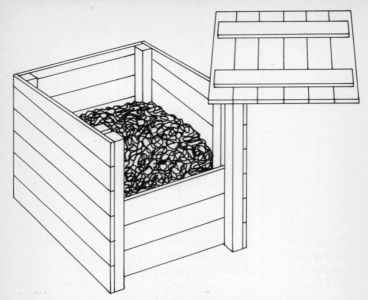

Fig. 2 *A sophisticated compost bin made from wooden slats and fitted with a removable sloping lid. Removable slats in front will allow you to dig out the compost easily.*

BUILDING THE HEAP

First put a layer of woody prunings or brushwood in the bottom, again to aid air circulation. Then build up the heap in 20 cm (8 in) layers, either all in one operation or over a period of time, depending on how much waste material the garden yields. An activator of some kind will speed up the composting process. This can be, for instance, dried blood, poultry manure, farmyard or stable manure, or a general organic fertilizer high in nitrogen. Sprinkle each layer with one of these.

All materials should be chopped up fairly small and, ideally, mixed together. Grass mowings, especially,

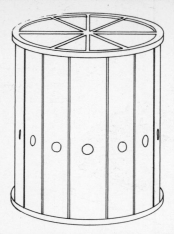

Fig. 3 *There are various proprietary compost bins on the market, many being ideally suited to small gardens. This popular type has sliding PVC panels to allow easy access to the compost, and the fitted lid prevents rain from entering. Holes in the sides allow air circulation within.*

should be well mixed with other materials otherwise they will pack down into a blanket-like mass and fail to rot. You can use any soft plant material on the compost heap, such as old bedding plants, hedge clippings, leaves, old stems of perennials, kitchen vegetable waste and weeds. However, do not use weeds containing seeds, nor the roots of perennial weeds like dandelions, stinging nettles and docks.

Woody prunings from shrubs, fruit trees, etc., may be used but they should first be chopped up into small pieces with a garden shredder (see p. 74). You can also use torn-up newspaper in moderation. And green-manure crops can also be composted (see below).

Do not put on the compost heap cooked food nor plants with diseases. Avoid using lawn mowings from the first cut after lawn weedkiller has been applied.

TURNING THE HEAP

When you have a reasonable heap of material it will heat up. As it is cooling down the heap should be turned, which speeds up the composting process. The material from the outside should be turned in to the centre and the inside material put on the outside of the heap to ensure the whole heap rots evenly.

MAKING LEAFMOULD

If you can collect enough fallen leaves in autumn, stack them in a heap (within a wire enclosure as for garden compost) and allow them to rot down until they crumble readily. This will take at least a year, or maybe two years.

You can use virtually any leaves but avoid those of evergreen shrubs and trees, like holly, laurel or pine. The best leaves are from beech and oak trees.

Leaves should be moistened before being placed on the heap. Firm each layer down by treading.

GREEN MANURE

This is a very cheap form of bulky organic matter. It involves sowing a special green manure crop, allowing it to grow and then digging it in to the soil before it becomes tough or sets seeds. Alternatively, it can be cut and added to the compost heap. Of course, green manuring is practical only if the plot of land is lying fallow. Normally it is recommended for the vegetable plot, sowing during summer as ground becomes vacant.

WHAT AND HOW TO GROW

You can use clover, lupins, mustard, radish (fodder type) or ryegrass. You may find other green-manure crops in seed catalogues. Seeds are simply scattered on the bare ground after raking it. The plants should be cut down and chopped up before digging them in.

MANURES IN CONCENTRATED FORM

Of course, using bulky organic matter presumes you have the ability to handle these often heavy materials, that you have the space to cope with them and that you can easily get outside materials into the garden.

If any of these are out of the question you have the option of proprietary concentrated manures or organic soil improvers, available in bags from garden centres or from specialist mail-order suppliers (these advertise in the gardening press). These products are especially recommended if you have a small garden.

As these have to be used more sparingly, perhaps because they are concentrated, or because they are cost-prohibitive when used in large volumes (always follow to the letter manufacturers' instructions on use) they do not provide the same bulk as the materials mentioned earlier. So they will not alter the soil structure to the same extent as bulkier materials will. However, some products do markedly improve the soil, certainly resulting in the formation of reasonable amounts of humus, and they contain plants foods, if not as much as fertilizers. You will find that some products are based on seaweeds, which are excellent soil improvers.

Some products contain peat, so do check on this if you want to avoid using peat products. Make sure, too, that the manure content was not derived from factory farms if you are against these production systems.

INORGANIC SOIL IMPROVERS

There are other materials of inorganic (non-living) origin that can be used for improving your soil, either during or after digging.

COARSE SAND OR GRIT

If you have a clay soil which drains slowly after rain, with pools of water lying on the surface, bulky organic matter alone may not be sufficient to cure the problem. Dig in a 5 cm (2 in) deep layer of coarse sharp sand or grit to open up the soil and allow rainwater to drain through more easily and swiftly. Both are obtainable in bulk from builders' merchants, and are also available in bags from garden centres – an expensive way to buy but possibly sensible for small-garden owners.

LIME

This is useful for adding to sticky clay soils – it improves their texture and makes them easier to cultivate. Sprinkle it on to dug ground during autumn and allow it to lie over winter, then fork it in. If manure has been applied while digging, wait a few months before applying lime.

Before considering the application of lime, however, carry out a soil test to see how acid or alkaline your soil is, as lime increases the alkalinity of the soil. Simple soil-testing kits are readily available from garden centres and shops, and will show the acidity or alkalinity of your soil measured on the pH scale.

Do not apply lime if you have lime-free (acid) soil and want it to remain acid for growing lime-hating plants. For an excessively acid soil, below pH5, some lime is recommended. If your soil is already quite alkaline, say pH8, then do not use more lime, as an excess can lead to problems. A pH of 6.5 to 7 is ideal for vegetables and many other plants.

If needed, use ground limestone or hydrated lime. The amount to apply will be based on the soil test and the test kit should supply a guide.

It is only necessary to apply lime to clay soils every five years, but sandy soils will need more frequent applications – every two to three years – as lime is quickly washed out by rain.

Instead of lime one can use calcified seaweed – which is like a type of coral and bought as a proprietary product – but it is more expensive. It also contains a number of minor plant foods.

GYPSUM

Gypsum (sulphate of lime) is an excellent material for applying to clay soils to improve their texture, reduce stickiness and make them more easy to cultivate. Unlike lime, gypsum does not increase the alkalinity of the soil so can safely be used on soils with a high pH. It is also ideal for acid soil if you do not want to increase the pH.

Gypsum is applied in the autumn after digging, as for lime. Apply at the rate of 226 g per square metre (8 oz per square yard).

BEFORE PLANTING

It has already been suggested that you thoroughly prepare the soil in beds and borders before planting, including digging and adding bulky organic matter and other soil improvers. However, for a long time it has been standard practice to add fertilized peat or other bulky organic matter to the planting holes for such permanent plants as trees and shrubs in the belief that this gets them off to a good start.

However recent research has found that there is no benefit at all in this practice, and that it is a waste of good materials. If the ground has been well prepared beforehand, that is all that needs to be done to give plants a good start in life.

It is much more beneficial to use this organic matter to provide the trees and shrubs with a mulch when planting is completed. A mulch suppresses annual weeds and helps the soil to remain moist during dry periods, both of which very much help in the rapid establishment of newly planted trees and shrubs. Competition from weeds actually retards the growth of young trees and shrubs.

TREES IN LAWNS

It is worth remembering that if you are planting a specimen tree in a lawn you should never allow the grass to grow right up to the trunk, at least for several years until the tree has made reasonable growth. Far better to leave a circle of soil about 90 cm (3 ft) in diameter around it and to apply a mulch to this.

The technique of mulching, and the best materials to use, are described on page 29.

CHAPTER 2

IN THE GREENHOUSE

The greenhouse is another place where heavy demands are made on peat. Until recently all seed and potting composts contained peat but now it is possible to buy peatless composts.

PEATLESS COMPOSTS

There is a dual-purpose seed and potting compost based on coconut fibre (see page 11). At the time of writing it is still very new but seems a very promising alternative to peat-based composts.

Coconut fibre is spongy, like peat, and holds on to moisture well, and it encourages good root growth. The compost contains plant foods but these last for only four to six weeks, after which plants should be fed every seven to fourteen days with a proprietary liquid fertilizer.

This compost can also be used for rooting cuttings, as an alternative to the traditional cutting compost of peat and coarse sand in equal parts.

The compost is also recommended for outdoor containers such as hanging baskets. And, of course, it can be used for growing all kinds of greenhouse plants, including tomatoes and other crops in pots.

OTHER COMPOSTS

Other new peatless composts are based on composted straw and sewage. There are also bark-based composts which consist primarily of bark but contain some peat. Bark is a waste product of the timber industry. Again it is advisable to start liquid feeding about four weeks after plants are established.

Rockwool (a mineral used for insulation) is being experimented with as a growing medium for plants. Currently it is possible to obtain a proprietary pack of rockwool blocks in various sizes in which to grow plants, together with a special fertilizer to feed them. This is soilless culture or hydroponics. You may like to carry out your own experiments with these blocks.

GROWING BAGS

Growing bags are widely used in greenhouses for growing crops such as tomatoes, sweet peppers or capsicums, aubergines, cucumbers, melons, lettuces and so on (Fig. 4). They are much better than planting in soil borders as the plants are isolated from pests and diseases in the soil and there are none of the problems that may be encountered when growing the same crop in the same border year after year, a practice which can result in extremely poor growth and a build-up of pests and diseases.

Growing bags are easy to use – simply place the bag on the greenhouse floor and cut holes in the top for the plants. A standard-size growing bag will comfortably hold three tomato or similar-sized plants, or two melon or cucumber plants.

When plants are established, in four to six weeks, carry out regular weekly or fortnightly feeding. As the bags do not have drainage holes one must be careful

Fig. 4 *It is now possible to obtain growing bags filled with peatless compost. They are ideal for growing tomatoes and other crops in greenhouses – better, in fact, than planting them in soil borders as the plants are isolated from soil-borne pests and diseases.*

when watering to avoid saturating the compost – bags do not dry out as quickly as pots. There are available special growing-bag crop supports, for one cannot use bamboo canes to support the plants.

At the end of the season the bag is thrown away, after spreading the compost on the garden.

Growing bags are mainly filled with peat-based potting compost but now bags filled with coconut-fibre compost are coming on to the market.

RING CULTURE

Ring culture is another excellent method of growing tomatoes and other similar greenhouse crops such as sweet peppers and aubergines (Fig. 5).

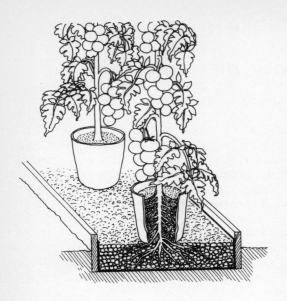

Fig. 5 *Ring culture is an excellent method of growing tomatoes and other similar greenhouse crops. The plants are grown in bottomless pots or 'rings' which are placed on a bed of horticultural aggregate or shingle. The plants are watered via the bed and fed via the rings.*

The plants are grown in plastic bottomless pots which are popularly called 'rings'. They are approximately 23 cm (9 in) in diameter. You could, alternatively, make your own rings by cutting out the bottoms of plastic pots with a hacksaw.

There are several benefits to be obtained when using the ring-culture technique. It isolates plants from pests and diseases which live in the soil. It ensures even uptake of water by the plants, thus avoiding the problem of erratic watering. It makes use of renewable materials, especially if the rings are filled with a peatless compost, such as one based on coconut fibre.

SETTING UP THE SYSTEM

The rings are set up on the greenhouse floor. If they are to be placed over a soil border, first cover the soil with a sheet of polythene. Next, put down a 15 cm (6 in) deep layer of aggregate, retaining it with an edging of timber planks. Aggregate can be washed pea shingle or a proprietary lightweight horticultural aggregate. This aggregate base can be used for several years in succession if flooded with water when the crop has finished to wash out any fertilizer residues. It should then be sterilized with a horticultural disinfectant to kill any pests and diseases.

The rings are placed firmly on the aggregate base, spacing them about 45 cm (18 in) apart each way, and then filled to within 5 cm (2 in) of the top with a peatless potting compost.

Plant the tomatoes or other plants and then water them well to settle the compost around the roots.

CARING FOR THE PLANTS

After this initial watering you should apply water only to the aggregate. This encourages the plants to root into the base. You will need to check the aggregate daily as it must be kept moist at all times.

You may now be asking how to support tall plants such as tomatoes, as the system will not support bamboo canes. Instead, use nylon strings. The lower end of a length of string is looped around the base of a plant, leaving plenty of room for stem thickening. The other end is tied to a taut horizontal wire some 1.8 m

(6 ft) above the ground The string must not be too tight, nor too loose, as it is twisted around the plant's stem as it grows, so providing support.

Once established, after four to six weeks, the plants are fed weekly via the rings, using a liquid fertilizer. A proprietary tomato fertilizer is good not only for tomatoes but other fruiting plants, too. One can obtain tomato fertilizer based on seaweed.

POTS FOR PLANT RAISING

It is a popular practice to raise plants in compressed-peat pots, or in peat modules which expand when soaked in water. The idea is that when transferring the plants to the garden they suffer no root disturbance, as the pot or module is planted with the plant, and it decomposes in the soil.

This technique is commonly used for various crops which are raised in the greenhouse for eventual planting in the garden, such as lettuces, sweet corn, outdoor tomatoes, marrows and cauliflowers. It can also be used for various ornamental plants like sweet peas, bedding geraniums and other summer-bedding plants.

A good alternative which you can make at home is the paper pot, made with rolled-up newspaper. Cut a double thickness of newspaper roughly into a square or rectangle, to the height of pot required plus an additional 5 cm (2 in). Roll the paper around a cylinder or tube of the diameter required for the pot, leaving the excess 5 cm projecting beyond the end of the cylinder. This 5 cm length of paper is then twisted and formed into the base of the pot, which should, of course, be flat. And that's it.

Obviously paper pots should not be handled too much after they have been planted, as they are not as substantial as peat pots.

SAVING ENERGY

A lot of heat can be wasted unnecessarily in the greenhouse. The heat loss through glass is tremendous and considerably increases fuel bills. You may be heating the greenhouse too much – consider using less heat, or avoid artificial heat altogether.

REDUCING HEAT LOSS

To reduce heat loss and therefore save energy and reduce heating bills it is essential to insulate a greenhouse.

The most popular way is to line it inside with bubble polythene greenhouse insulation. This consists of two sheets of clear polythene sheeting with air bubbles sandwiched between. This insulation considerably reduces heat loss and can reduce heating costs by up to 60 per cent. Bubble polythene is easily fixed to wooden-framed greenhouses with tacks, or to aluminium-framed houses with special fittings which are 'plugged' into the glazing bars. The insulation can be taken down in summer when the greenhouse is not artificially heated.

When installing the insulation material, leave a 1–2 cm (½–1 in) gap between it and the glass to create an additional insulating layer of air. The ventilators must not be sealed, but should be insulated individually. Likewise the door, of course!

USING LESS HEAT

Some plants, such as tomatoes and capsicums, and certain bedding plants like ageratum, begonias, pelargoniums ('geraniums') and scarlet salvias, initially need high temperatures, so consider buying them at planting time from a garden centre, rather than raising your own from seed. Instead raise hardier subjects in a cool greenhouse, with a minimum temperature of 4.5°C (40°F). At this temperature you could raise hardy vegetables for planting out in the garden, and you should also have success with some tender kinds such as sweet corn and marrows. Many of the hardier summer bedding plants can be raised in these conditions, including alyssum, antirrhinums, annual pinks, stocks, annual phlox, marigolds and zinnias.

Even if you do not heat the greenhouse at all you can still make it very productive. You can plant tomatoes, capsicums and aubergines in early summer. Use it in autumn and winter for pots and bowls of hardy bulbs such as daffodils, tulips and hyacinths, plus pots of polyanthus and winter-flowering pansies.

CHOOSING A HEATER

Without hesitation I recommend electric heating (such as a fan heater or tubular heaters, fitted with a thermostat) for the greenhouse, as electricity is the most efficient fuel, besides being non-polluting, reliable, automatic and convenient. However, it is not the cheapest fuel, initially will be costly to install and you will need a professional electrician to install the power supply, sockets and so on.

You will also need an electrically heated, thermostatically controlled propagating case for seed raising and/or rooting cuttings.

PART 2

PLANT CARE

CHAPTER 3

MULCHING

Mulching is a gardening practice whereby the soil around the plants is completely covered with bulky organic matter, shingle or a synthetic material. One of its purposes is to prevent rapid evaporation of moisture from the soil, resulting in less frequent watering being required during dry periods. So this saves water. Another reason for mulching is to prevent annual weeds from growing and it is therefore one of the alternatives to using chemical weedkillers.

A mulch should be laid on completely weedfree and moist soil. Apply fertilizer first. A mulch (except for black polythene or very heavy dense materials like old carpet) will not suppress perennial weeds like docks, dandelions or stinging nettles, so these must be removed, together with roots, before a mulch is laid. The usual time to lay a mulch is in spring. Permanent organic mulches may also be topped up at this time.

ORGANIC MULCHES

Bulky organic matter is particularly good for mulching as it also adds humus to the soil. Most types, however, provide shelter for slugs and snails so be on your guard for these pests. There are plenty of traditional and several 'new' materials to choose from.

THE NEWEST ORGANICS

One of the newest mulching materials is cocoa shell, a by-product of chocolate manufacture. It is very attractive in appearance, the broken shells being tan coloured, so it makes a very suitable mulch in ornamental parts of the garden. It has a rather rough texture so it repels slugs and snails. Cocoa shell adds plant foods to the soil – nitrogen, potash, magnesium and manganese – and it has a pH of 5.1, so it is acid. Cocoa shell is very light in weight, so it is easy to handle and spread, but when moist it holds down well. A 5 cm (2 in) layer is recommended for mulching.

Coconut fibre (see page 11), which resembles sphagnum peat, is also recommended. Again it is a lightweight, attractive-looking material and creates a pleasing effect in ornamental beds and borders. Lay it 5 cm (2 in) thick.

Bark makes an excellent mulch in the ornamental garden and is the longest-lasting organic material available. Partially composted bark is recommended, as is raw chipped bark for mulching. Surprisingly, bark is not a cheap material, despite the fact that a lot is produced by the timber industry. An 8 cm (3 in) layer will suppress annual weeds more effectively than the generally recommended 5 cm (2 in) layer.

A new proprietary bagged product for mulching, containing wood and paper residues (both composted and by-products from industry) is being widely acclaimed by gardeners and readily available from garden centres. A 2.5 cm (1 in) deep layer is recommended. Being good looking, it is ideal for the ornamental garden.

TRADITIONAL ORGANICS

Well-rotted farmyard or stable manure is a traditional mulching material but not particularly pleasing aesthet-

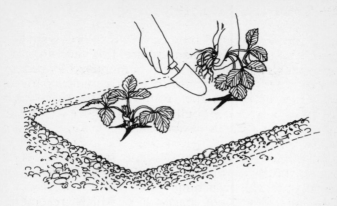

Fig. 6 *If strawberry plants are planted through a strip of black mulching polythene they will not be troubled by weeds and the fruits will keep clean. Bury the edges of the polythene in the soil and plant through cross-shaped slits.*

ically. Nevertheless it is often used on rose beds, and would be acceptable for mulching larger plants such as shrubs. It is also recommended for mulching fruits and vegetables. These manures also supply plant foods. A manure mulch should be spread 5–8 cm (2–3 in) deep.

The same comments apply to garden compost. A problem with both manure and compost is that they may contain weed seeds. If these are not killed during the composting process they will germinate after the mulch has been laid. So be prepared to do some hand weeding if using these materials.

Mushroom compost may also be used as a mulch in the ornamental or utility garden, spreading a layer at least 5 cm (2 in) deep. It is reasonably pleasing in appearance as it is well rotted. As mushroom compost contains chalk do not use it around lime-hating plants such as rhododendrons, camellias and heathers.

Leafmould can also be used for mulching and looks particularly good in woodland gardens and shrub borders. Leafmould may contain weed seeds, so once again be prepared for crops of weeds.

SHINGLE

Pea shingle is becoming more widely used as a mulching material and to create gravel areas. It is particularly effective when used around 'architectural' plants – in other words, groups of bold foliage plants, including grasses. Lay pea shingle 2.5–5 cm (1–2 in) deep. Pea shingle will help to keep the soil moist and suppress weeds but for even better moisture retention and weed control lay it over heavy duty black polythene sheeting. Make some holes in this with a garden fork to ensure drainage of rainwater and plant through cross-shaped slits.

A 2.5 cm (1 in) layer of pea shingle can also be used to cover the soil around a collection of alpines or rock plants, where it will give a more natural looking appearance than an organic mulch.

SYNTHETIC MATERIALS

Black mulching polythene (available in rolls from garden centres) is a widely used mulching material. It is not attractive so is generally used in the vegetable and fruit plot. However, it can be used in the ornamental garden but is then best covered with an organic mulch or shingle. Such a combination would give extremely good weed control (it will even suppress perennial weeds) and moisture retention.

If mulching individual fruit trees or bushes, place a 90 cm (3 ft) square of polythene around each one. For rows of vegetables lay a strip of polythene, wider than the row, and plant through it after making cross-shaped slits for the young plants. Potatoes can also be planted through black polythene, as can strawberry plants (Fig. 6). Lay strips of polythene between sown rows of vegetables or between rows of raspberries.

The edges of the polythene should be anchored by burying in slits made in the soil with a spade, or securing with bricks. It is best to make some small holes in it with a garden fork to aid drainage of rainwater.

Never throw away old carpet, for it makes a superb mulch in the vegetable or fruit plot. Use it in the same way as black polythene. It will even suppress perennial weeds, and when wet it becomes very heavy so will not need anchoring down.

CHAPTER 4

FEEDING PLANTS

These days many gardeners are turning to organic fertilizers, which are renewable resources, rather than manufactured types.

WAYS TO FEED PLANTS

Plants should be fed only when they are actively growing, which is spring and summer. However, having said that, it is a traditional practice to add an organic fertilizer to the soil prior to autumn planting, but one that is slow to release its plant foods.

BASE DRESSING

This is an application of fertilizer to the soil prior to planting or sowing. It is recommended for both permanent plants (such as shrubs) and prior to sowing or planting temporary kinds like most vegetables and bedding plants. The fertilizer is scattered on to the soil surface, at a rate recommended on the container, and forked or raked into the top of the soil. A base dressing may also be given to the compost in containers, such as patio tubs and window boxes, before planting temporary plants like summer bedding. Do not add fertilizer to plant containers filled with new compost, as this will already contain plant nutrients.

TOPDRESSING

This is an application of fertilizer around growing plants. Again it is scattered on to the soil surface and ideally incorporated into the soil by hoeing. Topdressings are mainly used to feed permanent plants like shrubs, roses, hardy perennials, fruit trees and bushes, a feed being given during early spring as growth begins. Generally a topdressing is not necessary around temporary plants if a good base dressing was given, although sometimes a supplementary feed may be needed in summer to boost growth.

LIQUID FEEDING

Liquid feeds are concentrated liquid fertilizers diluted with water according to the instructions on the container. They are ideal for feeding container-grown plants during the summer, and for feeding pot or container-grown plants in the greenhouse. Usually one starts feeding four to six weeks after planting. Several liquid fertilizers are organic, some being based on seaweed.

WHAT TO USE

The most convenient type of fertilizer is one which contains all the major plant foods – nitrogen, phosphorus and potassium. This is known as a compound fertilizer. It can be used as a base and topdressing.

One of the best known and most useful organic compound fertilizers is blood, fish and bone, which is reasonably quick in releasing its plant foods. Sometimes it contains very little potassium (look at the information on the pack to see what it contains), in which case it may be desirable to add extra to the soil in the form of rock potash.

FERTILIZERS SUPPLYING NITROGEN (N)

Some organic fertilizers supply mainly nitrogen, which is responsible for leaf growth. Dried blood is a well-known nitrogenous fertilizer and it quickly starts to feed plants. It is excellent as a topdressing to give a quick boost to vegetables in the summer. It is also ideal for lawns for quickly greening them up in spring or summer, although do apply at least annually a compound fertilizer.

Another well-known organic fertilizer supplying nitrogen is hoof and horn. This also supplies some phosphorus. It releases its foods slowly and is generally used as a base dressing, for shrubs or other permanent plants.

Fish meal contains quite a lot of nitrogen and a little phosphorus, plus some minor plant foods. It starts to feed plants fairly quickly and can be used as a top or base dressing.

FERTILIZERS SUPPLYING PHOSPHORUS (P)

Phosphorus is an important plant food as it encourages root growth and plays a big part in the formation of seeds and fruits. The best known organic fertilizer supplying phosphorus is bonemeal, which also contains a little nitrogen. It is slow to start feeding plants and is therefore mainly used as a base dressing, especially when planting permanent plants like shrubs and trees. Use sterilized bonemeal.

FERTILIZERS SUPPLYING POTASSIUM (K)

The third important plant food is potassium, which is responsible for development of flowers and fruits. The fertilizer generally recommended to environmentally friendly gardeners is rock potash, which is inorganic (it is a mineral which occurs naturally). This is slow to start feeding plants. It may be used in conjunction with other fertilizers, including blood, fish and bone if this fertilizer is low in potassium.

Also supplying potassium (and also some nitrogen) is seaweed meal, which is slow to start feeding plants. It also contains a number of minor plant foods. Can be used as a base or topdressing.

FEEDING PLANS

You will need some kind of programme or plan for feeding plants on a regular basis so this is summarized below, together with suggested fertilizers. For application rates, follow the directions on the packet.

VEGETABLES

★ Apply a base dressing of blood, fish and bone two weeks before sowing or planting vegetables. Alternatively apply hoof and horn, but add to it bonemeal and rock potash.

★ Leaf vegetables such as cabbage, Brussels sprouts, kale, lettuce and spinach, plus 'heading' types like cauliflower and broccoli, will benefit from a topdressing of nitrogenous fertilizer in summer when actively growing. Dried blood is recommended. Onions and leeks also appreciate extra nitrogen. Gardeners generally prefer to apply the recommended amount as as several small topdressings over a period of several weeks.

FRUITS

* Annually, in early spring, apply a topdressing of blood, fish and bone.
* Also in early spring each year apply rock potash, as fruit require a good supply of potash in order to produce heavy crops.

ORNAMENTAL PLANTS

These include roses, trees, shrubs, climbers, conifers, bulbs, hardy perennials, rock plants and spring and summer bedding plants.

* Apply a base dressing of blood, fish and bone before planting. Alternatively apply hoof and horn, but add to it bonemeal and rock potash.
* Annually, in early spring, apply a topdressing of blood, fish and bone.
* Bulbs benefit most from weekly feeds of a seaweed-based liquid fertilizer, from immediately after flowering until the leaves die down.
* Give roses a further topdressing of blood, fish and bone after the first flush of flowers.

LAWNS

* Apply top dressing of blood, fish and bone in the spring each year.
* If you feel that the lawn needs a boost in summer give a topdressing of dried blood, but not during dry or drought conditions
* Lawn topdressings should be watered in.

POTTED PLANTS

★ Give greenhouse plants in pots and other containers a liquid feed weekly or fortnightly during spring and summer. If newly potted/planted, start feeding four to six weeks after planting. Seaweed-based liquid fertilizers are particularly good.

★ Treat temporary plants in patio tubs, window boxes, hanging baskets and other containers in the same way. If compost has not been replaced with fresh, add a base dressing of blood, fish and bone before planting.

★ Permanent plants in outdoor tubs or other containers should receive a topdressing of blood, fish and bone in spring. If you feel they need a boost in summer, give several liquid feeds.

CHAPTER 5

WATERING PLANTS

With the concern over water shortages, and consequent bans on garden watering which seem to occur annually these days, it is important not to waste water. The prospect of water metering (it is already on trial) and more expensive water are further good reasons for conserving water.

There are numerous ways of reducing water consumption in the garden without the garden suffering, although be prepared for the lawn to go brown during prolonged dry periods or during drought. The lawn is the first thing many people water at the onset of dry weather in spring or summer; however, water can be put to better use. Once the rainy weather returns lawns recover surprisingly quickly even if they have turned as brown as cardboard. You will not have a tip-top lawn if it is allowed to go short of water, but today many environmentally friendly gardeners are prepared to forgo this.

Remember, when using a hosepipe connected to the mains water supply it is now a legal requirement to install a back-siphonage protection device to prevent water supplies from being contaminated.

KEEPING THE SOIL MOIST

You can drastically cut down on watering if you reduce the evaporation of water from beds and borders. The way to do this is to mulch the soil around plants. (This technique, and the materials used, is fully described on p. 29.) The most efficient material for keeping the soil moist is black polythene.

Also encourage the soil – especially very well-drained types such as gravels, sands and chalk – to hold on to water by digging in bulky organic matter (see page 9).

WATERING GARDEN PLANTS

If you decide to start watering, which should commence when the top 2.5 cm (1 in) or more of soil in beds and borders has become dry, you should decide which plants take priority – which are most at risk from drying out.

PLANTS AT RISK

Plants most at risk include newly planted trees, shrubs, roses, conifers, fruits and climbers, which are vulnerable for up to two years after planting.

Newly planted perennials are at risk for up to a year after planting.

Summer bedding plants must be watered for the first six weeks after planting if the soil starts to dry out, after which they should be able to tolerate drier conditions.

Also taking priority are plants growing hard up against walls, fences and hedges, or under large trees, where the soil is liable to be drier than in other parts of the garden.

Vegetables which take priority include such 'thirsty' types as runner beans, celery, lettuces, early potatoes, spinach and tomatoes. It may be better to avoid growing these if your area is prone to hosepipe bans.

HOW MUCH TO APPLY

Overall watering, using a garden sprinkler, is quite wasteful in some situations, but is sensible for all closely planted areas, such as beds of summer bedding plants or borders of perennials.

How much water should you give? Certainly enough to moisten the soil to a depth of at least 15 cm (6 in). To achieve this you will need to apply the equivalent of 2.5 cm (1 in) of rain. This is approximately 27 litres of water per square metre (or roughly 5 gallons per square yard). When watering with a sprinkler or hosepipe, you can measure the amount being applied by standing some tins or jam jars under the sprinkler. When they contain 2.5 cm (1 in) of water you know you have applied sufficient.

It is more economical to water plants individually. This is certainly feasible with larger plants such as shrubs, trees, conifers climbers and so on. Basin planting of these, whereby the plant is set in a shallow depression, will help stop water from running away, and it is more effective at catching rainwater. The amount of water to apply to a plant will depend on its size – say from 4.5 litres (1 gallon) for smaller plants to 18 litres (4 gallons) for larger plants. Apply slowly so that there is no overflow or run-off.

Evening is the best time to apply water as then there is little evaporation.

LAWNS

To help prevent the soil drying out too quickly give the lawn a topdressing each autumn of equal parts coconut fibre and coarse horticultural sand, at a rate of 1 kg per square metre (2 lb per square yard), brushing it well in.

During dry weather never mow closely – a cutting

height of 2.5 cm (1 in) is recommended. Mowing will be needed less often, anyway, as the growing rate of the grass will slow down.

CONTAINERS

Outdoor containers such as patio tubs, window boxes and hanging baskets will need checking daily for water requirements – even twice daily in very hot weather – as they can dry out rapidly. Hanging baskets, especially, are notorious for this.

Apply just enough water so that it starts to trickle out of the bottom of the container, which indicates the entire volume of compost has been moistened.

There is no doubt that containers take a lot of water, so if you feel they are taking too much then reduce the number.

GREENHOUSE WATERING

The same comments concerning outdoor containers also apply to potted plants in the greenhouse or conservatory.

The most economical way to water pot plants on greenhouse staging is to install a capillary watering system (Fig. 7). Basically this system, for which complete kits are available, consists of capillary matting which is laid over the staging. Plants in plastic (not clay) pots are then stood on it. The matting is kept constantly moist from a reservoir of water and the plants take up only the water they require. This system will also save you a lot of time and work.

Capillary systems should only be used during the spring and summer. It is better to rely on hand watering in autumn and winter when plants do not need so much

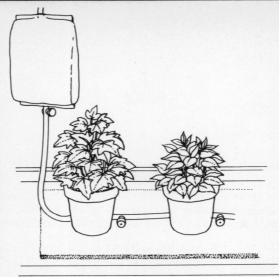

Fig 7. *The most economical way to water pot plants on greenhouse staging is to install a capillary watering system. The capillary matting can be kept moist by means of a drip watering system supplied from a water reservoir bag. With this method, the plants take up only the water they require.*

water and dry out less quickly.

Another way to save on greenhouse watering is to add a granular water-holding polymer to the compost during potting. This will ensure it dries out less rapidly, and is available from several mail-order garden suppliers.

COLLECTING RAINWATER

Rainwater collected from the house, garage and greenhouse roofs can be used for watering greenhouse plants, and outdoor plants, too, if you can collect enough. You can collect it in a modern plastic rainwater butt which is stood under a downpipe.

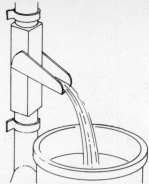

Fig. 8 *A good way of collecting rainwater is to fit a water-saving device to a rainwater downpipe. This directs the water into a butt and can be opened and closed as necessary.*

There are water-saving devices which can be installed in rainwater downpipes to direct water into a butt. They can be opened and closed as necessary (Fig. 8).

DROUGHT-RESISTANT PLANTS

If you live in a dry area and/or are subject to hosepipe bans, or you generally want to save as much water as possible, then look for more drought-resistant plants. These should survive dry periods and drought without watering, once they are well established. Examples include:

Hardy ornamentals: allium, anthemis, cistus, coronilla, cytisus, euphorbia, genista, gleditsia, helichrysum, juniperus, lavandula, olearia, perovskia, phlomis, robinia, rosmarinus, ruta, hardy salvias, sempervivum, spartium, teucrium, tulipa and yucca.

Drought-resistant vegetables include brassicas (cabbages, Brussels sprouts and relations); root crops like beetroots, carrots, parsnips, swedes and turnips; and leeks and onions.

CHAPTER 6

PEST AND DISEASE CONTROL

There are many pests and diseases which attack garden and greenhouse plants. There is an equally wide range of insecticides and fungicides to eradicate them. However, these pesticides can also harm or kill beneficial insects and other creatures. But take heart – if you decide to give up using pesticides there are numerous other methods of controlling pests and diseases which will not harm wildlife.

REMOVAL BY HAND

Larger pests, particularly caterpillars such as those of the cabbage white butterfly, can be picked off by hand and disposed of. Aphids (greenfly and blackfly) which congregate on shoot tips, can be squashed between fingers. Do, however, learn to recognize beneficial insects like ladybirds as these should not be destroyed, for they prey on pests (ladybirds eat aphids). Consult a well-illustrated book on insects to get to know what's what.

Slugs and snails can be picked up when seen and disposed of – not a pleasant job!

Diseased shoot tips and leaves for instance, shoots or

leaves covered in white fungal patches (powdery mildew), or leaves of roses covered in black spots (the notorious black-spot disease), can be removed from plants, provided there are not too many. Flowers or other parts of plants covered in grey fluffy fungus (grey mould) can be removed. Diseased material should be put in the dustbin, never on the compost heap.

TRAPPING PESTS

One of the latest ideas is the pheromone trap for trapping codling moths, which lay their eggs on apple trees – which results in maggot-ridden apples. The trap lures male codling moths to their doom with synthetic pheromone – the scent that females use to attract males – before mating takes place. Hang the traps in apple trees from late spring (Fig. 9).

Bands of sacking or corrugated cardboard tied around trunks and larger branches of apple trees in mid-summer will trap codling moth larvae. Remove and destroy in late autumn. Greasebands tied around apple-tree trunks in mid-autumn will trap winter moths, whose caterpillars eat leaves and buds. Remove in mid-spring.

Earwigs can be trapped in inverted straw-filled pots supported on bamboo canes. Position them among plants prone to earwig damage, like dahlias.

DETERRING PESTS

There are several methods of preventing pests from even reaching plants. Special fibre or felt collars fitted around the base of brassicas (cabbages, Brussels sprouts, cauliflowers and their relations) will prevent attack by

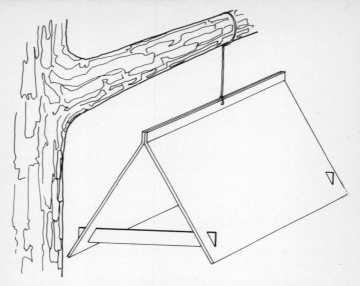

Fig. 9 *This trap lures male codling moths to their doom with synthetic pheromone – the scent that females use to attract males – before mating takes place. Hung in apple trees from late spring, it should ensure maggot-free fruits.*

cabbage root fly. Similar collars or mats are available for placing around strawberry plants to protect the fruits from slugs.

The floating cloche, perforated polythene sheeting, used to cover vegetables to promote better and quicker growth, will also act as a barrier to pests. There is also a lightweight fleece made from spun polypropylene which serves the same purpose. These barriers will safeguard vegetables from such serious pests as cabbage caterpillars, carrot root fly, cabbage fly, greenfly and blackfly.

Surround carrots with a 75 cm (30 in) high barrier of polythene sheeting, supported with corner posts, to prevent attack from carrot fly.

NATURAL PEST CONTROL

Today it is possible to buy parasites and predators which keep pests under control. These may be insects or other creatures and are available from specialist mail-order suppliers. This is known as biological control and at the moment is used mainly to control greenhouse pests. The parasites or predators are introduced into the greenhouse only when pests are established. Each type lives only on one particular pest – it will not attack any others nor harm plants.

BIOLOGICAL CONTROL IN THE GREENHOUSE

Several serious greenhouse pests can now be controlled biologically. There is a parasitic wasp (*Encarsia formosa*) to control glasshouse whitefly. Red spider mite can be controlled with a predatory mite (*Phytoseiulus persimilis*). An Australian ladybird (*Cryptolaemus*) is used to control mealybugs. Then there is a bacterium (*Bacillus thuringiensis*) which eradicates caterpillers. This can also be used outdoors. Dried spores of this bacterium are applied as a spray but they will not harm insects other than caterpillars. All parasites and predators come with instructions for use.

IN THE GARDEN

Biological control also takes place naturally in the garden, perhaps without your knowing: ladybirds, lacewings and hoverflies feed on aphids; aphids and caterpillars may be attacked by parasitic wasps; ground-beetles eat slugs and insects; and centipedes devour pests in the soil like leatherjackets. All of these 'friendly' creatures will thrive in a pesticide-free garden.

You should try to encourage other beneficial creatures, too. Hedgehogs eat slugs and various insects; toads and frogs have a similar diet; and many common birds are insect eaters. Further details of how to encourage wildlife into the garden will be found in Chapter 13.

RESISTANT PLANTS

Wherever possible choose plants which are resistant to diseases. Plant breeders are constantly producing new varieties of fruits, vegetables and flowers with disease resistance.

You should also aim to grow plants as well as possible, as a healthy thriving plant is better able to cope with an attack from a disease or pest. That means preparing the soil well prior to planting, and subsequently feeding and watering as necessary.

RESISTANT ROSES

Rose catalogues generally indicate if a variety is disease-resistant. We should be looking for varieties that are resistant to the three major rose diseases – blackspot, mildew and rust. However, you should remember that if these diseases are very bad in a particular year then even resistant varieties may succumb.

Examples of large-flowered (hybrid tea) roses that are resistant to these three are: 'Alec's Red', 'Blessings', 'Grandpa Dickson', 'Peace', 'Pink Favourite', 'Royal William', 'Silver Jubilee' and 'Troika'.

Cluster-flowered (floribunda) roses which are resistant to the dreaded three are 'Anne Harkness', 'Beautiful Britain', 'City of Belfast', 'Korresia', 'Lover's Meeting', 'Mountbatten', 'Southampton' and 'The Times'.

Resistant climbing roses are 'Aloha', 'Arthur Bell',

'Compassion', 'Dortmund', 'Galway Bay', 'Golden Showers', 'Joseph's Coat', 'Mme Grégoire Staechelin', 'Maigold', 'New Dawn' and 'Wedding Day'.

RESISTANT VEGETABLES

The following should be considered for their disease resistance. Bear in mind that this is not an exhaustive list by any means. Good seed catalogues will give many other examples. The disease to which the variety is resistant is given in brackets.

Greenhouse cucumber: 'Fembaby' (mildew), 'Pepinex' (mosaic virus); **lettuce**: 'Avondefiance' (mildew, also root aphids); **parsnip**: 'Avonresister' (canker); **pea**: 'Kelvedon Wonder' (mildew); **potato**: 'Maris Piper' (potato blight, plus eelworm), 'Pentland Javelin' (scab, plus eelworm); **swede**: 'Marian' (mildew and clubroot); **greenhouse tomato**: 'Estrella' (verticillium, fusarium, cladosporium and tobacco mosaic virus), 'Grenadier' (fusarium and leafmould), 'Piranto' (brown root rot) and 'Shirley' (fusarium, tobacco mosaic virus and cladosporium).

RESISTANT FRUITS

Like vegetables, fruits also have their fair share of troubles so try the following disease-resistant kinds. More should be found in the catalogues of good fruit specialists. The disease to which the variety is resistant is given in brackets.

Cooking apple: 'Newton Wonder' (scab); **dessert apple**: 'Sunset' (scab); **blackcurrant**: 'Ben Lomond' (mildew); **gooseberry**: 'Keepsake' (mildew); **pear**: 'Beurre Hardy' (scab); **raspberry**: 'Malling Leo' (spur blight, cane spot, plus aphids); **strawberry**: 'Red

Gauntlet' (grey mould), 'Troubadour' (red core, verticillium wilt and mildew).

HYGIENE

Maintaining hygienic conditions in garden and greenhouse goes a long way towards preventing troubles from pests and diseases.
* Never leave piles of rubbish lying around.
* Never allow weeds to become established.
* Avoid piles of materials like timber, plant stakes, pots. Keep them in a dry shed.
* Quickly clear fallen leaves.
* Dispose of any badly diseased plants.
* Maintain fresh airy conditions in the greeenhouse.
* Dig any vacant ground to expose soil pests.
* Wash pots and seed trays thoroughly before use.
* Always use fresh compost for sowing and potting.
* Wash the greenhouse thoroughly inside and out once a year in autumn, using a detergent.

CROP ROTATION

On the vegetable plot practise crop rototation which ensures that vegetables are grown in a different plot of land each year. This prevents a build-up of soil-borne pests and diseases. The rotation can be in a three-year cycle, as shown in Fig. 10.

RINGING THE CHANGES

As plants become old and start to decline they need to be pulled up and discarded. However, if you wish to

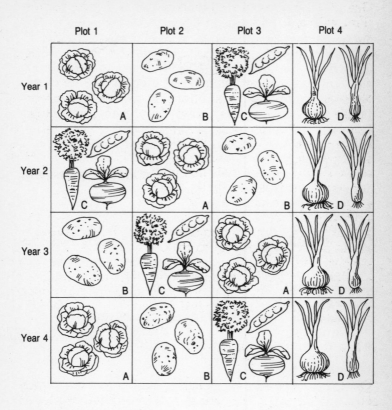

	Plot 1	Plot 2	Plot 3	Plot 4
Year 1	A	B	C	D
Year 2	C	A	B	D
Year 3	B	C	A	D
Year 4	A	B	C	D

Fig. 10 *Crop rotation in the vegetable plot prevents a build-up of soil-borne pests and diseases. A three-year rotation is normal and involves three plots with a semi-permanent fourth plot for asparagus, onions and leeks.* **A** *contains brassicas (cabbages and relations) and salad crops;* **B** *contains potatoes; and* **C** *contains root crops (carrots, etc.) and legumes (peas and beans).* **A** *should be manured and limed;* **B** *is manured but not limed;* **C** *should not be manured nor limed, but manure legume rows; and* **D** *should be manured.*

replant with new plants of the same kind they should never be set in the same place, as they may not establish due to a problem known as replant disease. Examples include roses, fruit trees and bushes, and strawberries. Instead choose another part of the garden. Completely different subjects can safely be planted in the site of the old plants.

MAJOR TROUBLES

Here is a summary of the most common pests and diseases, with methods of control:

Aphids: squash, biological, floating cloche.
Caterpillars: pick off, floating cloche, biological.
Grey mould: pick off affected parts of plant, hygienic conditions.
Leaf spot (roses): pick off affected leaves.
Powdery mildew: pick off affected leaves.
Red spiter mite: biological.
Slugs/snails: pick up, strawberry mats, hygienic conditions, digging.
Whitefly: biological.

CHAPTER 7

WEED CONTROL

What are weeds? The usual definition is a plant that grows where it is not wanted. The plants we regard as weeds are wild kinds which increase and spread vigorously, competing with our garden plants. Not all wild plants can be called weeds, though. Some are welcome in the garden, especially such charming and harmless kinds as primroses and cowslips.

There are two basic types of weeds. Annuals increase prolifically from seed. They complete their life cycle, from seed germination to flowering and seed production, in one growing season. Examples include annual meadowgrass, bittercress and chickweed.

Perennial weeds live for several or many years and often spread by means of creeping underground roots or stems, such as stinging nettles, ground elder and couch grass. Others, including docks and dandelions, have a long thick root called a taproot.

There are alternatives to chemical weedkillers in the battle to control weeds, but the first rule is to try and make sure you do not indirectly introduce weeds into the garden yourself.

Inspect plants before you buy them – there should be no weeds growing in the container. The annual weed bittercress has been spread around in this way – it is a prolific seeder and its seeds may be on or in the compost of the plant you purchase. But they are undetectable so there is nothing you can do.

NEIGHBOUR'S WEEDS

Another problem which is not of your making is the weedy, neglected neighbour's garden. Weed seeds may be blown into your garden and the creeping roots and stems of perennial kinds may find their way under the fence. Unfortunately there is not a great deal you can do to get your neighbour to maintain a weed-free garden. Obviously you should try a polite request, first by chatting to your neighbour and then, if that brings no response, by writing or – if your neighbour is unable to maintain the garden due to age or ill health – you might consider having a go yourself, with your neighbour's permission.

If the above moves fail, the local council may be able to do something. It would certainly be worth liaising with your council, especially if there are several complaints from people in the area.

To prevent the creeping roots or stems of perennial weeds from encroaching into your garden, create a barrier with polythene sheeting. Dig a narrow trench 30 cm (12 in) deep along the boundary, line one side of it with a strip of polythene sheeting, then return the soil.

CONTROLLING WEEDS

There are various ways of controlling weeds in ornamental beds and borders and on the fruit and vegetable plot.

HAND WEEDING

In small areas such as tiny beds, containers and rock gardens this is a practical way of getting rid of annual weeds. It simply involves pulling them out, first loosening them if necessary with a hand fork. Take care not to loosen cultivated plants. If you do, refirm immediately by pressing the soil all round with your fingers.

DIGGING OUT WEEDS

Perennial weeds growing among garden plants may be dug out individually, using a garden fork or spade. Some, such as docks and dandelions, have deep roots, perhaps going down to 60 cm (2 ft), so you will have to dig down deeply. Other weeds, like couch grass, stinging nettles and ground elder, have creeping roots or stems just below the soil surface; they quickly cover bare ground but are easier to dig out.

It is most important to remove every scrap of root or stem, for pieces left in the ground are capable of developing into new plants.

It is difficult to remove perennial weeds growing though the centre of hardy perennials or small shrubs. If this occurs, the only thing to do is lift the plant during the resting season, extract the weeds then replant.

The roots or stems of perennial weeds are easily removed during normal digging. This is the best way to prepare a weedy piece of ground for planting, and here double digging is recommended (see pages 10–11).

HOEING

One of the best, easiest and quickest ways of controlling weeds is to hoe them off during the seedling stage. You can hoe around plants in beds and borders and along rows of vegetables. Choose a warm dry breezy day when the surface of the soil is dry, then the weed seedlings will quickly shrivel and die.

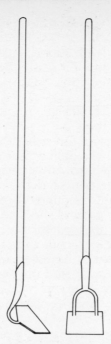

Fig. 11 *One of the easiest and quickest ways of controlling weeds is to hoe them off during the seedling stage. There are two types of hoe: the draw hoe (left), used with a chopping action, is ideal for hard or stony ground, and the Dutch hoe (right), used with a pushing action, is more suited to easily worked soils.*

There are two types of hoe you can use. The Dutch hoe is used with a pushing action, sliding the blade just below the soil surface, when it cuts off the weeds. Then there is the draw hoe which is used with a chopping action, ideal for hard or stony ground (Fig. 11). There is a hand (short-handled) version of this called the onion hoe, excellent for working between closely planted crops, etc.

COVERING THE GROUND

Covering the ground will suppress the growth of annual
weeds (perennials, too, if a really dense, light-excluding
material is used). Mulching (see p. 29) is one way of
covering the ground.

If you want to eradicate perennial weeds from
unplanted ground, then cover the ground with black
polythene or old carpet for at least one year.

Once they have completely covered the soil with
stems and leaves, low growing ground cover plants will
suppress annual weeds. Use dense-growing plants and
plant close together. Ground cover can be created
among larger plants such as shrubs, on banks instead of
grass or indeed in any part of the garden where you
want weed-free conditions but an attractive effect. As this
is a big subject it cannot be covered thoroughly in this
book, so if you are interested obtain a copy of *Ground
Cover Plants* by Janet Browne (Concorde Gardening
series, published by Ward Lock).

WEEDS IN LAWNS

If you maintain a really dense healthy lawn with no bare
or thin patches, few weeds will be able to establish.
Achieving this means regular attention to feeding,
watering, spiking or aerating, topdressing and raking,
and avoiding mowing too closely. (For these aspects of
lawn maintenance you will need to refer to a book on
lawns.)

Any weeds that do appear, particularly such common
rosette-forming kinds as daisies, dandelions and plantains,
will have to be dug out by hand. There is available a
special tool for this known as a daisy grubber. Re-seed
resulting bare patches. Other weeds, the mat-forming
kinds such as clover and yarrow, are not easy to remove

without the use of a chemical weedkiller, so are best left and in any case they are not too conspicuous.

MOSS

Moss is also difficult to remove without chemicals. Indeed, if you rake out live moss you will only spread it and make the problem worse. However, you will need to rake out established moss (together with dead grass) and this is best done in summer when it may be dead, using a wire lawn rake or, for large lawns, a powered lawn rake. If this results in a thin sward, scatter grass seed over it and keep watered if necessary until it germinates.

The best solution is to try to prevent moss from establishing. This again means creating a dense healthy sward as mentioned above.

Certain conditions encourage moss: shade, damp and very acid soil. Try not to site a new lawn in a shady spot – you could replace a permanently shady part of a lawn with shade-loving ground-cover plants.

If drainage is poor, aerate or spike the lawn several times each year, using a garden fork, or a mechanical aerator for large lawns. Once a year, in autumn, use a hollow-tine aerator which removes cores of soil, followed by a topdressing with sharp horticulural sand.

If the pH of your soil is below 6 you may need to apply lime (see page 18).

PART 3

GARDEN FEATURES AND PLANTS

CHAPTER 8

MISCELLANEOUS FEATURES

Wherever possible try to create garden features with renewable materials, especially if they are available locally. For example, in many areas hit by the severe gales of recent years there is still plenty of timber lying around which could be put to good use in the garden, although never take any timber without the owner's permission.

STEPS

Sections of tree trunk 23–30 cm (9–12 in) thick and up to 60 cm (2 ft) in diameter make excellent steps for a steep bank. They should be set one above the other, slightly overlapping (rest the edge of one on the edge of another), recessing them into the bank and with the tops perfectly horizontal. Before setting the trunk sections in place, first remove the bark and then treat them with a horticultural wood preservative, as this will considerable lengthen their life.

There is one problem with log-section steps and that is they can become very slippery in wet weather, especially if moss or algae are allowed to form on them. Therefore, regularly clean the treads by scrubbing them, using water and detergent. I find that a light scattering of coarse sand or fine dry soil helps to ensure a non-slip surface.

Steps can also be made with sections of tree branches or thin tree trunks about 90 cm (3 ft) in length (Fig. 12). Again, they should first have the bark removed and then treated with a horticultural wood preservative. The logs are held in place with wooden stakes at each end, rammed well into the ground in front of them – chestnut fencing posts cut to length are ideal and should be treated with timber preservative.

Either one or two logs will be needed for each riser (the vertical parts of the steps), depending on their thickness. Do not make risers too high or the steps will be difficult to ascend. Risers should be about 15 cm (6 in) high but they can be up to 23 cm (9 in). The treads (the parts that you walk on) should be a minimum of 30 cm (12 in) deep and preferably up to 45 cm (18 in) deep. Steps should have a minimum width of 90 cm (3 ft).

The treads are simply formed of well-rammed soil. To make this more stable and hard you could mix some dry cement into the surface of the soil before firming it. The cement will then harden and bind the soil together. Another idea is to surface the treads with chipped bark. This will not stabilize the soil but will prevent the treads from becoming muddy and slippery in wet conditions, and will stop moss and algae from forming.

PATHS

Sections of tree trunk about 15 cm (6 in) thick also make excellent paths if they are placed in the form of stepping stones, their tops level with the surrounding ground. However, if the stepping 'stones' run through a lawn they should be set just below the soil surface so that the lawn mower can run over them. Once again, first remove the bark from the trunk sections and treat them with horticultural wood preservative. As with

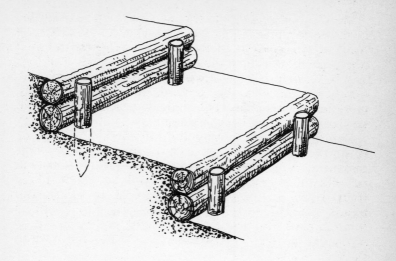

Fig. 12 *Unwanted timber can often be put to good use in gardens. Sections of tree branch or thin tree trunks make excellent steps and can be held in place with wooden stakes. The treads are simply formed of well-rammed soil.*

wooden steps, take precautions against slippery surfaces (see page 61).

Paths can also be made with a coarse grade of chipped bark. This can be laid direct on to well-rammed soil and should be about 8 cm (3 in) deep. An edging made with rough-sawn timber will prevent the bark from spreading. This can be supported by nailing it to timber posts rammed into the ground on the inside edge. Again, all timber must be treated with a wood preservative. If available, branches cut to length make a suitable edging (see page 66).

RAISED BEDS AND BORDERS

Raised beds and borders are very popular in garden design today as they create a variation in height. This is quite important, of course, in today's small flat plots.

Raised beds or borders can be built direct on level ground and may be 45–60 cm (18–24 in) in height. However, you may prefer less height, especially if you want a long raised border. In this instance the height could be between 15 and 30 cm (6–12 in). Fill the beds or borders with locally purchased topsoil.

Traditionally raised beds and borders are built up with bricks, natural walling stone or concrete walling blocks, but why not try timber – a renewable resource?

RAILWAY SLEEPERS

Timber railway sleepers are excellent for creating raised beds. These are no longer being made as modern railway sleepers are formed of concrete. Timber sleepers are heavy and best used for low raised beds or borders. They can be set on edge and sunk 5–8 cm (2–3 in) into the ground for stability. Timber posts inserted behind them and nailed to the sleepers will ensure extra stability.

It is possible to buy imitation railway sleepers and these can be stacked one on top of the other to create raised beds and borders. They can be secured by driving timber posts into the ground behind them and bolting the sleepers to them.

VERTICAL LOGS

It is possible to buy vertical 'logs' which are supplied in rolls, and these are excellent for creating raised beds or borders. They are available in heights of 15, 30 and 45 cm (6, 12 and 18 in). The half-round pales (made from plantation-grown timber and treated with preservative) are joined together with metal strapping and each section can be joined to the next. The sections should be sunk about 5 cm (2 in) into the ground to prevent movement and the soil firmed well around them. If you want extra rigidity, ram timber posts into the ground on the inside and nail the sections to them.

SITTING AREAS

Sitting areas are traditionally made from natural-stone paving, concrete paving slabs or bricks but if you want to use a renewable material why not consider chipped bark? This makes a very soft surface and is suitable, too, for surfacing a children's play area. For these uses lay the bark about 10 cm (4 in) deep.

Another idea is raised timber decking. You may be able to buy ready-formed decking, in which case simply lay it on bricks or concrete building blocks to slightly raise it above the ground. The bricks or blocks should be concreted into the ground for stability.

You could make your own timber decking from old floorboards – perhaps obtained from a demolition site or builder's yard. Each joist (supporting beam) is again supported on bricks. This, of course, is a project for the DIY enthusiast.

EDGINGS

Straight sections of tree branches or thin tree trunks make ideal edgings for beds, borders and bark paths or sitting areas. In some parts of the country there is still plenty of timber just lying around.

Simply lay the sections end to end to form an edging, sinking them about 5–8 cm (2–3 in) into the ground for stability and then firm the soil around them. Some people prefer to leave the bark on, but eventually it will part company from the timber.

Such an edging looks particularly good in informal gardens where you want to create a 'rustic' atmosphere.

CHAPTER 9

PLANTS AND THEIR CONSERVATION

Digging up plants from the wild for cultivation in gardens has been going on for years and is still taking place today in various parts of the world. For instance, wild bulbs are being dug up in their millions in southern Europe and Asia Minor. We gardeners must try to make sure we do not buy plants which have come direct from the wild, but it is not easy.

BULBS FROM THE WILD

It may seem a harmless enough pastime planting bulbs. However, some readily available kinds may have been dug up from their natural habitats in the wild. It is a fact that millions of bulbs of various kinds, including galanthus (snowdrops), miniature hardy cyclamen, narcissus (daffodils), anemones (windflowers), eranthis (winter aconites), sternbergias and leucojums (snowflakes), which are native to southern Europe and Asia Minor, are dug up from the wild every year.

This, of course, is having a very serious effect on wild populations and some bulbs are on the verge of extinction in the wild. Why is this done? It makes a source of income for poor local villagers. However, attempts are being made to encourage villagers to propagate their native bulbs for export, rather than exhaust the wild supply. If this can be carried out on a larger scale, then everyone, from villagers and conservationists to gardeners, should be happy.

BUYING BULBS

In the meantime we should be extremely cautious about buying certain bulbs in garden centres, supermarkets and from mail-order bulb specialists. It is bulb *species* (such as *Galanthus elwesii*, *Sternbergia lutea* and *Cyclamen hederifolium*), not hybrids, that are likely to have been dug from the wild. Be wary if there is no indication of their origins. Packets may also carry misleading information, like 'Produce of Holland', which may just mean that wild bulbs have been processed and packed in Holland. At the moment this trade in wild bulbs is poorly controlled, so let us hope that eventually legislation and controls will be considerably tightened.

How can we be certain we are not buying bulb species dug from the wild? The best bet is to buy from a mail-order bulb specialist who states in the catalogue that the bulbs listed have not been dug from the wild but raised in nurseries or gardens. This has led to some species having been deleted from certain catalogues, examples being sternbergias (those beautiful autumn-flowering bulbs with yellow, crocus-like flowers), some miniature narcissus and *Galanthus elwesii*).

Let us hope that more nurserymen will have a go at raising bulb species – some are very easy from seed, and there are also various modern propagation techniques that could be used.

Hybrids and cultivars (varieties) – in other words, those which have English names rather than Latin names – such as the large-flowered daffodils, tulips and hyacinths, are raised under cultivation so you should have no qualms about buying these. In any case, they are the most popular kinds of bulbs as far as the average gardener is concerned. But having said that, the species are rightly popular and there is no doubt that they are charming additions to gardens, especially rock gardens.

OTHER WILD PLANTS

Of course, collecting from the wild does not only apply to bulbs. All over the world plants are dug up from their natural habitats and end up in gardens. We have all heard stories of orchids being smuggled out of the tropics and even cacti being rustled.

Even in Britain certain plants are on the verge of extinction in the wild, or depleted to a few colonies, due to past collecting. Fortunately it is illegal to dig up many wild plants and bulbs. Populations of snowdrops, *Galanthus nivalis*, and wild daffodils, *Narcissus pseudo-narcissus*, for instance, are now few and far between. Bluebells are still quite a common sight in woods, possibly because they increase rapidly.

Always buy these bulbs from specialists as they are easy enough to propagate artificially – there is no need for anyone to raid the wild for such bulbs.

Some ground orchids are on the brink of extinction in the wild: the beautiful *Cypripedium calceolus* (lady's slipper) whose midsummer flowers have a light yellow lip and maroon petals, is just one example. Ground orchids are extremely difficult to increase under cultivation and wild-collected plants invariably fail to establish in gardens.

The wild cowslip, *Primula veris*, once very abundant in grassy places, is not seen as frequently these days. In the past it was dug up for gardens, being well-loved for its scented yellow flowers during mid- to late spring.

The same comments apply to the primrose, *Primula vulgaris*, with charming pale yellow flowers brightening woodland floors throughout the spring. Both of these are easily raised from seeds and fortunately today it is easy to buy nursery-raised plants for our gardens.

It is indeed a good idea to grow native species in our gardens to save them from extinction – but only if they have been raised in nurseries or gardens.

PICKING WILD FLOWERS

Some people make no secret of the fact that they pick wild plants and flowers for floral arrangements: such as berries in the autumn, autumn leaves, the seed heads of wild clematis, and so on.

I believe that wild flowers and plants are there for all to enjoy and not for the benefit of a few flower arrangers. Supposing this idea caught on – the countryside would be ruined in no time. Fortunately the majority of people grow their own material for cutting and arranging.

In Part 5, a number of native shrubs and other plants have been recommended for planting in gardens to encourage insects, birds and other creatures, but all are readily available from nurseries.

PLANT STEALING

There are still numerous cases that come to light of people stealing plants, or cuttings of plants, from gardens open to the public and from garden centres. Often these people are very keen gardeners and will stop at nothing, it seems, to obtain the plants they want. I have seen plants completely devoid of shoots where people have been taking cuttings as they pass by. I know of cases where choice orchids have been stolen from collections, and I once saw an elderly lady equipped with polythene bag and secateurs taking cuttings from plants in a botanic garden!

On being caught, some people have commented that they didn't think taking the odd cutting here and there was stealing. But it is. The plants are there for all to enjoy (and they have owners) so let us hope this kind of behaviour soon becomes a thing of the past.

PART 4

SAFETY AND COMFORT IN THE GARDEN

CHAPTER 10

SMOKE AND NOISE

It is all too easy for activities in the garden to affect the environment and to annoy the neighbours. Smoke from bonfires and noise from people and machinery are probably the two things that cause the most problems.

The latest outdoor trend is the barbecue but generally smoke and smells from this do not give cause for concern. It is unlikely a barbecue would be in use for any length of time. However, do consider your neighbours if you decide to have a 'barby' – keep it well away from the boundary and house and extinguish it as soon as cooking is completed.

BONFIRES

There is nothing worse than someone lighting a bonfire on a beautiful sunny day when others are relaxing in their gardens. Bonfire smoke not only pollutes the environment but can also be harmful to humans – the dense choking smoke produced by trying to burn green garden rubbish contains a high amount of cancer-causing chemical.

If a bonfire is absolutely necessary then wait until evening, make it only of quick-burning, dry garden rubbish, and make sure the weather is calm. Never light a bonfire when conditions are tinder dry during a drought – somebody living near me once set an orchard alight by having a bonfire during a dought period. Never burn other materials like polyurethane, which gives off lethal fumes. Keep the bonfire well away from houses, fences, trees and shrubs. Contain it in an incinerator. Remember that in many areas there are by-laws which allow bonfires only during a certain time of day. Never allow smoke to drift across the highway – this, in fact, is illegal.

PUTTING A STOP TO BONFIRES

If bonfires are a real problem – if a neighbour lights up frequently during the daytime, or if a fire goes on for hours on end – then you should first try to get the person concerned to ease up, first verbally and then if necessary in writing. If this is to no avail contact the environmental health department of your local authority with a view to getting the department to act on your behalf. It will help if several people get together to complain. The department will, of course, need concrete evidence, but they will advise on this. You must be able to prove that the bonfires regularly spoil your enjoyment of or prevent you from using your garden.

An alternative, which can be expensive and time-consuming, is to take the matter to court yourself. First, however, consult your solicitor or citizens' advice bureau. Most people would prefer not to go this far.

ALTERNATIVES TO BONFIRES

Much garden rubbish can be turned into valuable compost for improving the soil (see page 13).

Woody garden rubbish like fruit-tree, rose and shrub prunings cannot be composted unless it is first shredded, otherwise it would take a long time – years, in fact – to rot down.

Fig. 13 *Woody garden rubbish is best shredded in a garden shredder rather than burned; it can then be put on the compost heap, ultimately to be returned to the soil. There are various makes and models of garden shredder, powered by electricity (shown here) or petrol.*

If you have much woody rubbish it would be well worth investing in a garden shredder (Fig 13). These machines really do chop up woody rubbish finely, rendering it ideal for inclusion in the compost heap.

There are various makes and models available, from lightweight to heavy duty machines. The former are rather slow in operation but are fine for owners of small gardens who have comparatively little woody rubbish. The more expensive heavy duty machines are rapid in action, being designed for gardeners who have a great amount of material that needs chopping up. There are both electric and petrol shredders, the latter being more powerful and rapid in operation than electric versions.

Garden shredders are easy to use – you simply push the woody material into a hopper where it is chewed up by pulverizers.

Any garden rubbish which is not suitable for the compost heap, such as roots of perennial weeds and woody prunings (unless you can chop them up in a shredder), should be bagged up and taken to the local council tip. Indeed this is the best idea for all garden rubbish if you do not have room for a compost heap. Such disposal is completely free and it is therefore surprising that more people do not make use of this facility.

KEEPING THE NOISE DOWN

We live in a noisy world. There is endless traffic roaring by many houses and maybe aircraft overhead. There is often little we can do about this (but see Muffling Outside Noise, pages 76–77), but we should certainly do all we can to ensure minimum noise from our gardens, as most neighbours find noise very irritating.

NOISY MACHINERY

Petrol-driven machinery like lawnmowers is very noisy and is most intrusive in areas of high-density housing with small gardens. In this instance it is sensible to use electric machinery. Petrol-driven machinery is more practical for large gardens, and as houses are likely to be more spread out the noise becomes less noticeable.

NOISY PEOPLE

People can make a lot of noise, especially if they are having a party in the garden. Courteous people will let the neighbours know if they intend to have a large outdoor get-together – and perhaps invite them, too. They will hold it at a civilized time and not let it go on into the night, nor have blaring music.

Children can be noisy, especially when several are playing together in the garden. Even so one should try to keep the noise down and certainly not let it go on for too long. I once lived near a large family who disrupted the whole of the immediate neighbourhood, as the children often made a great deal of noise for very long periods.

Dogs barking for long periods also constitute anti-social behaviour. There is really no need for this if they are trained properly at an early age.

COMPLAINING ABOUT NOISE

If the noise is unbearable, frequent or goes on for long periods you are justified in making a complaint. Usually the best way is to have a polite word with the people concerned. If it still goes on confirm your concern in writing.

If this has no effect you should adopt the same procedure advocated on page 73, regarding putting a stop to bonfires.

MUFFLING OUTSIDE NOISE

Noise from outside the garden, such as that made by traffic and passers by, can spoil one's enjoyment of the garden. However, it may be possible to muffle or reduce this noise by dense planting along the garden boundary. Such a planting can also be used to shut out ugly views beyond the garden and, what is more, helps to give the impression of extra depth in the garden – particularly useful if your plot is on the small side. This is because the boundary will eventually be completely hidden and you will therefore feel that you can walk through the dense planting and find more garden beyond.

There are many ornamental shrubs which can be used to create a dense planting scheme. Plant them informally in bold, irregular groups. If they are backed by a solid panel fence the barrier will be even more effective at muffling noise.

CHAPTER 11

MACHINERY AND EQUIPMENT

There are many power-driven tools which can be a great help in the garden, saving hours of time and effort. But unless they are used properly and protective clothing worn if necessary, they can result in injury. Consider carefully the type of machinery you buy as some types are more environmentally friendly than others.

The major piece of advice I want to offer here is to read manufacturers' instructions on use and to follow these instructions to the letter. Remember to buy and wear any protective clothing the manufacturers recommend.

PROTECTIVE CLOTHING

When using machinery and equipment you should wear appropriate protective clothing. Surprisingly few people think of protecting their eyes, yet injury can be prevented simply by wearing goggles, especially when using power tools like a hedge trimmer, nylon-line trimmer, brushcutter, chainsaw or electric drill. Always wear goggles when using a garden shredder. It is also a good idea to protect your eyes when pruning, to prevent injury from twigs, and when chopping logs or sawing wood.

PROTECTING YOUR FEET

Surprisingly, too, many people do not think of protecting their feet when using machinery and equipment. You should wear really stout leather boots, ideally with reinforced toecaps, when using a motor mower, rotary cultivator, nylon-line trimmer, brushcutter, chainsaw or when digging (especially when using a fork).

OTHER PROTECTIVE CLOTHING

When using machinery never wear loose flowing clothing and dangling things like scarves and pendants as there is a possibility these may become caught up in the machinery. For the same reason, a hat would be sensible if you have long hair.

If you intend using noisy machinery for any length of time you should wear ear protectors.

Some people wear gardening gloves all the time. But when are they really necessary? Thick leather gardening gloves are strongly recommended when pruning as it is all too easy to cut your hand when using secateurs. Of course, gloves are essential when pruning thorny plants like roses. Stout leather gauntlets are advised when using a chainsaw or hedge trimmer.

HANDLING MACHINERY

Here is some safety advice to bear in mind when using machinery. Never use a motor mower on a bank. Some people use a hover mower in this situation, but even this is not recommended. Instead use a nylon-line trimmer or, better still, cover the bank with decorative ground cover plants instead of grass to provide a maintenance-free area.

Before using a motor mower always remove stones and any other debris from the lawn. All rotary mowers can fling stones some considerable distance and with great force.

If using an electric mower the cable should be slung over one of your shoulders. If you need to attend to the mower for any reason, always stop the engine or motor and, in the case of an electric mower, remove the plug from the socket. With a rotary mower wait until the blades have completely stopped rotating before attending to the machine.

TRIMMERS

With nylon-line trimmers sling the electric cable over your shoulder. Never raise the trimmer (nor a brush-cutter) above ground level – it is intended for cutting down weeds, long grass and the like, *never* for trimming shrubs or hedges. Before use, try to remove all debris such as stones and twigs as these can be catapulted and may then cause injury. Always make sure the machine is fitted with a guard. If you need to attend to the machine switch it off first and never get your hands near the rotating head until it has completely stopped spinning.

ROTARY CULTIVATORS

Sensible precautions to take here are not to use the machine on banks or other steeply sloping ground for fear of it tipping over. If the ground slopes slightly, then cultivate along the slope, not up and down it. First remove from the soil surface any large stones, bricks, pieces of wood or anything that is likely to foul the blades.

HEDGE TRIMMERS

A hedge trimmer, whether electric or petrol driven, must be used with the greatest care. Never swing it around wildly and never raise it above your head. If, you have a tall hedge to cut, stand on a secure stepladder. Always keep your fingers and long hair well away from the blades when in operation. An electric cable should be slung over a shoulder. Never cut a hedge when the leaves are wet.

When in use, hold the hedge trimmer with *both* hands, and make sure your feet are *firmly* on the ground or stepladder. Never walk around or move from one position to another when the machine is running.

CHAINSAWS

I am not going to give any safety advice here, for you should never use a chainsaw unless you have been properly trained by an expert. Chainsaws are potentially lethal weapons in inexperienced hands and I am amazed when I see people casually using them without any sort of training – and wearing no protective clothing! This was a common sight in my area after the severe gales of recent years.

County horticultural colleges often run courses on the use of chainsaws. A supplier may also be able to advise you on courses.

The average gardener probably won't need a chainsaw – if you have some trees which need felling or large branches to remove, you should never undertake these operations – always employ qualified tree surgeons.

NON-POLLUTING MACHINERY

Electric machinery is quieter than petrol-driven machinery, is lighter in weight and does not pollute the environment. It is not as powerful as a petrol-driven equivalent but is generally perfectly suitable for small to medium-size gardens.

Owners of large gardens may well opt for more powerful, speedier petrol-driven machinery; this should if possible be run on unleaded petrol. There should be no problem with new machinery. Remember that if the machine has a two-stroke engine, two-stroke oil must still be added to the petrol. If the machine has previously been running on leaded petrol make sure it will run on unleaded but first have the engine cleaned (decarbonized).

ELECTRICAL SAFETY

These days a lot of garden equipment is powered by electricity. This has numerous advantages: it is clean, quiet and the machinery is light in weight. However, we all know that electricity can be lethal and therefore has to be used sensibly.

RESIDUAL CURRENT DEVICE

It is highly recommended that you fit a residual current device (RCD) when using outdoor electrical equipment. This cuts off the electricity supply to the equipment (in hundredths of a second) should you cut through a cable or something else goes wrong, so saving you from electrocution.

There are various makes and models of RCD, from

the simplest portable type that is plugged into the socket like an adaptor, to a more permanent device which makes safe the whole household's electricity.

SAFETY RULES

Here are some simple rules to follow when using electricity in the garden:

* Plugs and cable connectors should be waterproof, and the cables designed for outdoor use.
* Never use an appliance if the cable is damaged or loosely connected to the plug.
* Do not use electrical machinery and equipment when it is raining and do not use a hedge trimmer when the hedge is wet.
* When using electrical equipment wear rubber-soled boots.
* Always keep the power cable well away from the cutting end of machinery or equipment – usually it proves safest to sling it over one shoulder.
* If you have to attend to the equipment, first switch it off and remove the plug; this is especially important if the cable has been damaged.

CHAPTER 12

PROBLEM PLANTS

Parts of some ornamental plants, such as berries, are poisonous and should not be eaten. This does not normally concern adults but parents should warn children of any dangers or keep a close eye on very young children. An even better idea would be to avoid growing poisonous plants. If a child does swallow part of a plant, contact your doctor immediately and show him or her a sample of the plant.

Some people are allergic to certain plants: simply touching the leaves results in rashes and irritation of the skin, or painful swellings.

POISONOUS PLANTS

Children are more likely to eat berries rather than other parts of plants such as leaves. Some garden plants with poisonous berries include ivy (*Hedera*), holly (*Ilex*), juniper (*Juniperus*), mistletoe (*Viscum*), cotoneaster, cherry laurel (*Prunus*), daphne (also has poisonous leaves), privet (*Ligustrum*) (leaves also poisonous), yew (*Taxus*), spindle (*Euonymus*) (leaves also poisonous) and the popular indoor pot plant, winter cherry (*Solanum*).

Plants that need special mention include laburnum (golden rain tree) which produces its seeds in pods. These look like mini pea pods and so children may well be tempted by these. They are very poisonous, as are all parts of the tree. Sweet peas may seem harmless enough but like the laburnum the seeds are contained in 'tempting' pods and are poisonous.

Children may also be attracted by the spikes of orange-red berries of lords and ladies or cuckoo pint (arum), a low-growing perennial with arrow-shaped leaves, native to Britain.

POISONOUS LEAVES

I have already mentioned some plants above with poisonous leaves, in connection with harmful berries. However, one should also be aware that some other popular garden plants have poisonous foliage. In particular beware of foxgloves (*Digitalis*), box (*Buxus*), monkshood (*Aconitum*) (all parts of plants are poisonous) and hellebores (*Helleborus*) which include the Lenten and Christmas rose. It is unlikely that children will eat the leaves of such plants – but you never know.

A potentially very harmful plant is the dumb cane (*Dieffenbachia*), a popular houseplant with large variegated leaves. The sap contained in the leaves and stems will cause severe inflammation if it comes into contact with the mouth and the victim will also temporarily lose his/her voice – hence the common name. So if you are pruning this plant, removing leaves or even propagating it from cuttings, do be very careful. Keep your hands well away from your face and wash them thoroughly afterwards. It is best not to grow this plant if you have young children.

PLANT ALLERGIES

There are numerous plants to which many poeple are allergic. Simply touching them may result in rashes and irritation of the skin and painful swellings. The best advice is not to grow any plants you know you are allergic to.

A plant which many people are allergic to is the pot plant *Primula obconica*. The leaves of this winter- and spring-flowering plant cause rashes.

Many people are also allergic to the leaves of *Rhus typhina* (stag's horn sumach) and to those of other species of rhus. This is a large shrub with big ferny leaves and it is grown primarily for its autumn leaf colour.

Some people may also suffer allergies induced by the leaves and stems of chrysanthemums whether the dwarf pot varieties for home decoration all year round, as plants for flowering under glass or as hardy herbaceous plants for borders. Some people may be allergic to the leaves of tomatoes and rue (*Ruta* graveolens).

If you grow poinsettias (*Euphorbia pulcherrima*), popular around Christmas time – those plants with the big scarlet leaf-like bracts – bear in mind that some people can be allergic to the sap, which may be exposed if you are removing leaves, and certainly if you are cutting back the plants after flowering. Other species of euphorbia, both tender and hardy kinds, may also have the same effect on some people.

PART 5

WILDLIFE

CHAPTER 13

ATTRACTING WILDLIFE

Do your bit for wildlife conservation by creating some conditions in the garden which attract birds, insects, amphibians, small mammals and other creatures.

A NATURAL HEDGE

Virtually all garden owners could create a natural hedge which encourages wild birds to nest and roost, and provides food for them in the form of berries. It could be created along a boundary or as a means of dividing a garden.

A natural hedge will not look out of place in a suburban or town garden. However, it must not be trimmed hard or you will lose many of the berries. A natural hedge is very much an informal feature.

Native shrubs should be used and planted in a mixture, spacing them 45 cm (18 in) apart in a line. Choose subjects like *Crataegus monogyna* (hawthorn) with red berries in autumn, deciduous; *Ilex aquifolium* (common holly), also with red berries if male and female plants are grown, which persist into winter, evergreen; *Rosa canina* (dog rose), red hips in autumn, deciduous; *Sambucus nigra* (elder), black berries, deciduous; and *Viburnum opulus* (guelder rose), red berries in autumn . (All these berrying shrubs of course have the added attraction of flowers, too.) If space permits, plant one or two small berrying trees in the hedge, like *Sorbus aucuparia* (mountain ash).

Wild honeysuckle (*Lonicera periclymenum*), with deliciously fragrant flowers, can be allowed to scramble through the hedge, providing berries for birds.

As a finishing touch sow wild flowers suitable for hedge bottoms, collections being available from wild-flower seedsmen.

WILDLIFE POND

A pond will attract all kinds of wildlife: newts, frogs, toads and water-loving insects like dragonflies. Birds and small mammals will use it for drinking, too, if the edges of the pond shelve gently.

The pond should be created in an open sunny position, slightly sunken and with grass right up to the water's edge. Making and planting a pond, although not difficult, is fairly involved, so if you are interested please refer to another book in this series: *Small-garden Pools* by Philip Swindells.

PLANTING

The pond should be well planted. Include some submerged oxygenating plants or 'water weeds' to help keep the water clear, like water violet (*Hottonia palustris*), milfoils (*Myriophyllum* species) and common fish weed (*Lagarosiphon major*).

A small water lily planted in the centre of the pond will help to shade the water – aim to have about one-third of the water surface covered with water-lily leaves.

Marginal plants should be grown in the shallow water around the edge of the pond. These can include British natives like the yellow flag iris (*Iris pseudacorus*); the lesser bulrush or reed-mace (*Typha angustifolia*), with brown sausage-like flower spikes; and the common rush (*Juncus effusus*). All water plants can be planted in special lattice aquatic baskets.

In the moist soil around the edge of the pond plant bog and moisture-loving plants such as marsh marigold (*Caltha palustris*) with yellow flowers; greater spearwort (*Ranunculus lingua*), yellow flowers; purple loosestrife (*Lythrum salicaria*), red-purple flower spikes; and globeflower (*Trollius europaeus*), yellow flowers like large double buttercups.

Some plants will be available from garden centres; others from a water-garden specialist.

WILD-FLOWER MEADOW

A wild-flower meadow attracts butterflies, bees and other insects and makes a delightful garden feature. It consists of long grass with various British wild flowers growing in it.

The meadow is best created from a special grass seed and wild-flower mixture, available from selected seed suppliers.

There are various mixtures suited to different soil types. One for a limy soil might contain ox-eye daisy (*Leucanthemum vulgare*), white flowers; lady's smock (*Cardamine pratensis*), delicate lilac flowers; meadow buttercup (*Ranunculus acris*), yellow flowers; daisy (*Bellis perennis*), white flowers; wild white clover (*Trifolium repens*), white flowers; field scabious (*Knautia arvensis*), blue flowers; and cowslip (*Primula veris*), yellow flowers.

A mixture for a lime-free soil might include the harebell (*Campanula rotundifolia*) with bell-shaped blue flowers, and the yellow-flowered bird's-foot trefoil (*Lotus corniculatus*).

The grasses themselves often have conspicuous flowers and might include quaking grass (*Briza media*), meadow barley (*Hordeum secalinum*) and crested hair-grass (*Koeleria gracilis*).

CREATING THE MEADOW

Choose an open yet sheltered sunny site for a wild-flower meadow. Ideally the soil should not be too rich, or the wild flowers will be dominated by the grasses.

Start from a completely fallow weed-free site. You cannot create a wild-flower meadow from an existing lawn as the grasses will be unsuitable, and besides it will be difficult to sow the seeds. The site should be dug, firmed and levelled. Rake the soil until it is fine enough for sowing.

The best time to sow the grass-seed/wild-flower mixture is early autumn; alternatively choose early to mid-spring. Sow thinly, at a rate of 25 g per square metre (¾ oz per square yard). Scatter the seeds on to the prepared seed bed and lightly rake them in.

AFTERCARE

When established, cut the meadow in midsummer and again in early autumn, to a height of 5 cm (2 in). Use a nylon-line trimmer and rake off the grass. That's all there is to it. A wild-flower meadow makes quite a labour-saving feature.

CORNFIELD

This is an area sown with the types of annual wild flowers which were once found in cornfields. It makes a colourful garden feature and attracts butterflies, bees and various other insects.

Typical summer-flowering cornfield flowers include the field poppy (*Papaver rhoeas*) with scarlet flowers; corn cockle (*Agrostemma githago*), red-purple flowers; cornflower (*Centaurea cyanus*), blue flowers; corn marigold (*Chrysanthemum segetum*), yellow daisy flowers; scentless mayweed (*Tripleurospermum maritimum*), white daisy flowers; and heartsease (*Viola tricolor*), yellow and purple flowers. Seeds of all of these are available from wild-flower seedsmen. You should be able to buy a cornfield mixture.

CREATING THE CORNFIELD

Choose an open yet sheltered sunny position where the soil is not too rich. Prepare it as for the wild-flower meadow (see page 91). Sow the seeds in the spring, scattering them on to the prepared seed bed and lightly raking them in.

Thereafter the plants should sow themselves, so there should be no need for further sowings in subsequent years.

BUTTERFLY PLANTS

There are many garden plants (as opposed to wild flowers) which also attract butterflies. One of the best known is *Buddleja davidii*, popularly called the butterfly bush, a large shrub covered in later summer with long spikes of honey-scented flowers in shades of blue, purple, red, pink or white according to variety. The ice plant (*Sedum spectabile*) and its varieties, is another plant to which butterflies are attracted in great numbers. It is a shortish hardy perennial which produces

Fig. 14 *Numerous garden and wild plants attract butterflies, which come to drink the nectar. Butterflies you can expect to see in gardens include (a) small tortoiseshells, (b) red admiral (c) brimstone, (d) peacock and (e) painted lady.*

flat heads of pink flowers in late summer and autumn.

Other garden plants which will bring butterflies into your garden include Michaelmas daisies or asters, heliotrope, sweet Williams (*Dianthus barbatus*), scabious, lavender and hebes.

Butterfly plants should be grown in a sheltered position as butterflies do not like windy conditions. They also like the sun, so choose a sunny spot.

If lots of butterfly plants can be grown together, so much the better. Small plants such as ice plants, sweet

Williams and Michaelmas daisies should be grown in bold groups as they will then be more effective at attracting butterflies.

It is very unlikely that butterflies will breed in the garden – this takes place in the countryside. However, you will be able to enjoy them drinking nectar from your flowers (Fig. 14).

MORE FOOD FOR BIRDS

Many birds are attracted to gardens by berries and seeds. I have already given a selection of berrying shrubs on page 88, but here is a selection of berry-bearing plants for the mixed border: barberry (*Berberis*), cotoneasters, crab apples (*Malus*) firethorn (*Pyracantha*), *Sorbus* species, deciduous *Euonymus* (spindle) and dedicuous viburnums.

The seeds of the following plants are relished by some birds: yarrow (*Achillea*), sunflower (*Helianthus*), globe thistle (*Echinops*), honesty (*Lunaria annua*), cornflower (*Centaurea*) and golden rod (*Solidago*).

It is a good idea to leave seeds on all permanent garden plants, like hardy herbaceous perennials, if you want to attract birds.

INDEX

Page numbers in *italic* refer to the illustrations

Acid soil, 18–19
Alkaline soil, 18–19
Allergies, 86

Bark, 11–12, 22, 30, 63, 65
Bedding plants, 27–28, 38, 41, 42
Biological pest control, 49–50
Birds, 88, 93
Blood, fish and bone, 35–36
Bonemeal, 36
Bonfires, 72–73
Bulbs, 38, 67–69
Butterflies, 91–93, *92*

Capillary watering, 43–44, *44*
Chainsaws, 81
Clay soil, 9, 18–19
Clothing, protective, 78–79
Cocoa shell, 30
Coconut fibre, 11, 21, 30
Compost, 12, 13–16, *14–15*, 31, 73
Composts, peatless, 21–22
Conservation, 67–71
Containers, 34, 35, 39, 43, *44*
Cornfield plants, 90–91
Crop rotation, 52, *53*
Cuttings, 21, 70–71

Digging, 9–11, *10*, 57
Drainage, 18
Drought-resistant plants, 45

Edgings, 65–66
Electric heating, 28
Electricity, safety, 82–83
Energy saving, 27–28
Equipment, 79–84

Feet, protecting, 80
Fertilizers, 21, 26, 34–39
Fish meal, 36
Fruit: disease-resistance, 51–52
    fertilizers, 38
    mulches, 31, 33

Gloves, 80
Green manure, 16–17
Greenhouses, 21–28, 39, 43–44, *44*
Grit, 18
Ground cover, 59
Growing bags, 22–23, *23*
Gypsum, 19

Hanging baskets, 21, 39, 43
Heating greenhouses, 27–28
Hedge trimmers, 81
Hedges, 87–88
Hoeing, 57–58, *58*
Hoof and horn, 36
Hops, spent, 12
Humus, 9, 17, 29
Hygiene, 52

Inorganic soil improvers, 18–19
Insulation, greenhouses, 27

Lawns, 62
    fertilizers, 36, 38
    planting trees in, 20
    watering, 40, 42–43
    weeds, 59–60
Leafmould, 12, 16, 32
Lime, 18–19
Liquid feeding, 35

Machinery, 75, 79–83
Manure, 12, 17, 30–31
Meadows, 89–90
Moss, 60
Mowers, 80–81
Mulching, 20, 29–33, 41, 59
Mushroom compost, 12, 31–32

Nitrogen, 35, 36
Noise, 75–77

Organic matter, 9–17

Paper pots, 26
Paths, 62–63
Peat, 5, 9, 17, 20, 21
Pests and diseases, 29, 46–54
Phosphorus, 35, 36
Poisonous plants, 84–86
Polythene mulches, *31*, 32–33
Ponds, 89–90
Potassium, 35–36, 37
Pots, paper, 26
Potted plants, 39, 43, *44*

Railway sleepers, 64
Rainwater, 44–45, *45*
Raised beds, 64–65
Residual current devices, 82–83
Ring culture, 23–26, *24*
Rock potash, 37
Rockwool, 22

Roses, 38, 50–51
Rotary cultivators, 80

Safety, 78–83
Seaweed, 17, 19, 37
Shingle mulches, 32
Shredders, *74*, 74–75
Shrubs, 20, 77–78, 88–89
Sitting areas, 65
Smoke, 72–73
Soil improvement, 9–20
Steps, 61–62, *63*
Supports, ring culture, 25–26

Theft, 70–71
Tomatoes, 22–26, 28
Topdressing, 35
Trees, 20
Trimmers, 80

Vegetables: crop rotation, 52, *53*
    disease-resistance, 51
    fertilizers, 37–38
    mulches, 31, 33
    watering, 41, 45
Vertical 'logs', 64–65

Watering, 5, 25, 40–45
Weeds, 20, 29, 55–60
Wild plants, 69–70, 89–91
Wildlife, 87–93